THE
ESSENCE OF
TIME

13TH & JOAN

For permission requests, write to the publisher, addressed "Attention: Permissions Coordinator," 205 N. Michigan Avenue, Suite #810, Chicago, IL 60601. 13th & Joan books may be purchased for educational, business or sales promotional use. For information, please email the Sales Department at sales@13thandjoan.com.

Printed in the U. S. A.

First Printing, August 2022.

Library of Congress Cataloging-in-Publication Data has been applied for.

ISBN: 978-1-953156-62-4

THE
ESSENCE OF
TIME

STEPHEN G. NORMAN

Contents

Tribute to Crystal

I have been blessed to watch Stephen grow into the young man he is today. As the youngest and the only boy of three, he has always moved to his own beat. He was uniquely bought into this world after our mother suffered two miscarriages with two girls after me and God saw fit to bless our parents with Stephen. I watched my little brother close but from afar and his motives were never to be a follower. I will not say he is perfect but by the grace of God he has turned out to be a solid young man with a drive that will motivate anyone to do better. As one of his older sisters, he has motivated me to pick up a lot of dreams I had pushed away due to working. I have never judged or told Stephen what to do or how to live his life: like every young adult, lessons have to be learned because without them we cannot grow. With all the interactions and situations Stephen faced while in college, he was still able to stay focused and graduate on time to become the first in our family to graduate from a university. As I read the poems, I begin to reminisce on his life and begin to think about how he overcame it all with his head held high. I am not only proud to call you my brother but also proud to know this young black man has not allowed stereotypes to inhibit his life."

                                          –Crystal R. Norman

To my sister Crystal, continue to watch over me beloved, for it was you that encouraged me to share this publication.

Secondly, I want to dedicate this body of work to anyone that is looking to turn their trauma into triumph by lessening the uneasiness of expressing their feelings towards their life experiences. To anyone who wants to stop running from their healing and yearns to understand who they are in order to evolve into their greatest selves.

Epigraph

"Just know that time heals
the hurt, but it also hurts to
heal."

-Stephen G.

"When will we realize that
time is a valuable vendetta
of the world?
Volunteering vengeance,
time unmasks individuals.
Facing flashbacks are painful,
needing to cleanse a thing
or two.
Remember that time you
were feeling vulnerable, it
took time to get close to
you."

-Stephen G.

Foreword: Who Is This Masked Man

We are presently living in a world where the wearing of a mask has become prevalent in one's daily walk of life. Yet, let me introduce you (the advent reader) to Stephen Norman, who, although he adorns the mask as well, has taken the time to write and hopefully enlighten his eventual readers that are seeking to be endowed with Stephen's well founded visionary and accumulated knowledge that may help each of you in your continued walk in this new and unpredictable life. My experience and endless adventures with the well-educated Stephen Norman were not just coincidental. Although his primary skills center around his Bachelor's degree in Athletic Training, Stephen's therapeutic stretching business *Tranquility Therapeutics, LLC* which offers primary relief of muscular retention throughout the human body, has successfully enabled him to stimulate a spiritual, physical, emotional, and mental cohesiveness within the human body. Stephen's attributes are a never-ending curiosity and thirst to venture and explore all the unknown elements he envisions that will invariably benefit those who chance to read this printed publication. There should be nothing less than excitement felt by charismatic readers once they possess this publication.

-*James D. Brown, Sr.*

Introduction

No one can prepare you for the emotional rollercoaster of interacting with diverse energies when entering a new stage in your life; well for me it was going to college. You can never be advised on your journey because each path is different. We have one thing in common though; we are all searching for the answers, the question reflects your own existence. *The Essence of Time* embodies a body of work predicated on the lessons and experiences I have endured. I view time as a double-edged sword because as much as we crave for it, we also abuse and take it for granted. The gift that keeps giving is to enjoy the moment as it happens, but to be completely consumed by that moment of time is a curse. I had so many questions as I was coming into my own modus operandi.

Writing helped me escape reality. Throughout undergrad I did not know I had anxiety; I felt deprived even though I was excelling but I could not get past the feeling that I was running in place. Self-sabotaging my greatness because I felt like I was not worthy of my light. To be aware of your pain and loss is beneficial, teaching you how to value who you are and to appreciate everything you do have. On another spectrum, lusting for validation is ignoring the very essence of your being. What's stopping you from accepting your truths?

Truth

If this truth is real...

Then I'd swallow the pill to
conceal,
Trapping the devil's tail from
hell.
Letting my spirit prevail.

My truth is no different from
yours,
Only time will tell.

Semester

Visine to keep my eyes clear,
do not mistake them for
tears.
Looking at my future it's a
celebration, so we light up
for our best years.

Semesters getting shorter;
ABC stores getting run
through.
Long semesters when you
are running through women
with bad intentions.
ABC's on your transcript.

Man listen, if I take one more
shot of that devil in the
bottle.
Going too fast, stepping
on the gas full throttle,
unpredictable moments.

Late nights getting ahead
were the motive,
but late nights getting some
head was picture perfect.

50/50 chance catch a
glance at the hourglass,
these times don't last.

Caught up in that fast line, is
it worth it?
Breaking all your axles asking
God to tow it.
Open your eyes before you
blow it.

You know you are a king
because your actions show
it.
Live and direct; lights,
camera action.
Hella views on my life, watch
my story on Snapchat.

Distractions

Distractions come in all
shapes and fashions.
Lashing out mental distress,
fasting from success.

Cracked image, breaking
any facades.
The realest form against all
odds.
Thank you, God, for saving
me from those frauds.

Reflecting when I was
paying tuition,
My vision was blocked by
promiscuous women.
Conflicted by lips and hips
but I remained driven.
Quick to hit then dismiss all
my feelings.

I cannot lie, pussy used
to have all my time and
devotion.

Watching out for women
being mischeivous.
Overtime facades fade out;
she could be feeling you but
at night letting other people
thieve it.

Distractions come in all
shapes and fashions.
Lashing out mental distress
fasting from success.

Chasing women is a
distraction; compelled
actions usually never
happen.
So I chase the assets that
attract them.
Ass, tits are attractive, but
your intellect and how you
perceive the world is the
main factor.

Expectations

Expectations will have your
mind racing,
Thoughts switching lanes,
to sustain the stains of
expecting different things
from human beings.

Expecting diminishes hope,
Suffocating your time and
fatal destruction to your
mind.

Tripping on any situation
playing the victim.
Detach yourself from those
suppositions,
assumptions giving you ill
intentions.

Why are you so defensive?
Blind eyes tell no lies, why
are you in feelings?
Don't you get tired of
playing the victim?

Carpe diem, pursuing past
pain ponder deepens.
Conscious defends the
perception of time,
Conditioned from systems
you must recondition your

mind.

We love to expect and lose
sight.
Yeah, we love to expect to
see side eyes from behind.
Overthinking is a threat to
your psyche.
Really, what do you value
inside?

Expectations will have your
mind racing.
Thoughts switching lanes,
to sustain the stains of
expecting different things
from human beings.

Deception

Deception sends you in the
wrong direction,
No question, life's lesson:
read the message.

His two cents are never
needed;
How could someone be
deceiving for no reason?
Never lenient, believe it's the
worst experience.

Sets a fence to trap the truth.
Living life with no absolute
means feening to lie.
Not accepting any reproofs.
He's waterproof to your
tears; deceit is a foul smell in
the air.

Decent man turned rotten
cold hearted.
Always bothered from the
real; reeling the feeling of
being counterfeit.
He dips and dabs adding
the frauds in being
fraudulent.

Deception sends you in the
wrong direction,

no question, life's lesson:
please read the message.

Can I Live?

The pain from the past is not
allowing me to unwrap my
presence.
Stress has me breathless, so
I undress that fine woman
with the big breasts.
Giving CPR to old flings still
wouldn't change things.

I mean, can a young n****
live?

Monday through Thursday
I'm stressing over classes.
Friday and Saturday the
alcohol has me on my ass,
and Sunday morning waking
up like what happened?

God, I know that you see
that I am trying to make a
difference,
Bank account hit the minus;
the refund went in an instant.
Spending on unnecessary
high's just to get by.

I cannot tell you how many
L's I've received,
Stuck in a place where I
don't want to be.

Sinning has me paralyzed
mentally.
N**** envy me because they
see what I don't see in me.

See, the old me died off and
I don't know this new ****.
He's chasing hoes, finessing
those just to collect their
souls.
Hitting the freak, while he
was hitting those freaks.
Week after week, the devil
has been on a consistent
streak.

This world is crooked you
must overlook it,
stay true to yourself and live
life to the fullest.

Manipulation

Manipulation is a real
manipulative mother fucker.

Mothers cannot control her;
She grows rebellious, college
freshmen trying to get her
credits.
Has her own crib, working
hard paying off her credit.

Telling her home girls her
business from the n****
she's finessing.
Perimeter distance, he's
traveling different nights just
to hit it.

Paying her bills, living lavish
from everyone she comes in
contact with.

Fix your contacts; catching
you slipping, finding time,
strategically planning ways
to take advantage.

Look how she maneuvers
in a manipulative manner,
holding you down putting
you at a disadvantage.

Attending all the parties and
attending all her classes,
testing people on a daily basis.

Manipulation is the man you
see finessing everybody for
money.

Smooth talker, crafty bastard,
Father wasn't there early on,
learning shit backwards.

Have his Master's in the
school of hard knocks,
knocking n****s out and
counting his money faster.

Waves 360 spinning,
manipulating women for the
sex, never stressed.

Fresh dressed pop eyes
when hitting the scene.
Always controlling the
outcome; come out of
situations never worried.

Look how he maneuvers in a
manipulative manner,
holding you down putting
you at a disadvantage.

He didn't attend class, hoop
dreams conflicted between
dropping dimes and making
cash.

Dismissed from his cases,
testing people on a daily
basis.

Manipulation is a real
manipulative mother fucker,
fucking the world without a
rubber.

Greed

The depths of hell cannot
cover your debt for real.
Thefts in jail are
contemplating their time to
prevail.
Distressed from the arrest,
deep breaths to inhale.

Claustrophobia in a cell
because they failed.
 Temptation nailed their
hands over dollar bills.

We cannot build judgment;
the feeling of worrying,
wondering where the funds
went.
Disabling us to function.

The tangibles of worldly
possessions are affecting
your budget.
Questioning where the love
is, but it didn't come from
your pockets.
Open your eyes quickly
before there's conflict.

Don't be obnoxious; the
greed of money can make
us all nauseous.
Nonchalant with withdrawals,
it'll cause deposits to rotten.

Identity War

Smooth persona keeping
my composure.
Life is a bitch, but I will not
divorce her.
Since '95 December 31st, it
makes sense that I was born
with a purpose.

Project buildings were my
pyramid,
had the sense to project my
rights to live.

Born where n****s are
known for indulging in
power.
Steal; kill just to advance in
territory from terror
Reminiscing when aunt Terra
gave me knowledge from
her era.

Views from an adequate
adolescent who couldn't
stay calm through the
calamities.
Walking in my soles size
thirteen.
Soul searching to find the
real me.
Trials and tribulations

resemble a symphony with
no need for sympathy;
refined my strategy.

Shaping my character can't
crack my exterior.
Reflecting on the man in the
mirror.
Silhouette abstract feeling
superior.
Flashback to the energy of
my ancestors.

The drought is alive but I'm
still reigning.
Disrespecting my rights can
bring famine.
Identity wars, Identity wars,
Identity wars.
Royalty is what I'm claiming.

Ungrateful

I'm contemplating my
spiritual being on this earth,
It is a gift and a curse.
Negativity compels to
disburse,
On a young king, you've
heard it first.

Burst of anxiety forced me
to hide behind facades;
Overanalyzed, failed to pick
a side.

Besides, I'm flirting with sin
by putting my hand up her
skirt.
Lusting for anything until you
are cursed,
Remapping your destiny,
rerouting your course.

Of course, we have options
to make the right decision.
The real lesson is to accept
the test and learn from it.
My homie Jazz told me that
when I was about to spaz
from the blues.

Trying to cruise with no
control.

Note 2 Self

If you love me then why do
you mentally abuse me?
Overthinking and drinking to
put you out of your misery.
Nah, you're really not feeling
me.

If you love me then why do
you allow others to take
advantage of my time?

Because each second of
the minute passes by and
becomes hours.
Days underestimate weeks
feeling weak; months
surrendering to the years.

Seeking reassurance and
ceasing the moment.
Put an end to the disowning,
realize the real and peep for
the phonies.

Phone in perfect reception;
left you on read but I'm sure
you received the message.
Don't question, just accept
it, stay strong and maintain
leverage.

Subconscious

Lost While Driving.
Tears falling from my eyelids,
negative thoughts eclipse
my consciousness.

Confined to the abyss of the
mind.
Where lips cannot witness,
travel the distance to see
what life defines.

Loneliness is the homicide
of time.

To suture my past,
It was fear that was holding
me back.

It took some time to master
my mind.
Though I was blind the light
illuminates inside.

To contemplate what has
been on my plate, no longer
the fear of fate.
Is it healthy?

To focus on wealth and
feelings never felt.
Imperfections used as bait

finding beauty in those traits.
Could you relate?

Bases loaded, baggage on
shoulders,
Why do you carry dead
weight?
Leave your problems at
wake.

Why are you second
guessing?
Wasting God precious
seconds, guessing who
would put you second.

Transitions

I'm going through phases,
phases, phases.
The lows just don't faze me,
faze me, faze me.
Embracing the highs while
chasing green faces,
I'm going through phases,
phases, phases.

Life's adversity has taken
a hold on me, but I didn't
learn those lessons at
university.
Woe is me, frozen dreams;
couldn't pitch ideas to my
reality.

Lost identities of
generational kings,
Millennial dreams of
centennial peace.
Adrenaline increases
equivalent to the feeling of a
million past criminals free;
But the cost of living isn't
free.

Catch a glimpse of how life
is played.
Never flinching, benched
pressed pressure adversity
you can catch this fade.

Transitioning through mazes;
Spiritual essence amazes,
to defend your natural
correlation.
Debating your blues while
questioning your views,
Patience is a virtue but
waiting can really hurt you.

Metamorphosis fused with
intuition,
Tortuous ride on the road to
wealth and riches.

We're going through phases,
phases, phases.
The lows just don't faze us,
faze us, faze us.
Maintaining the highs,
society can't change us.
We're going through phases,
phases, phases.

Growing Pains

Massage some wisdom into
her consciousness.

Subtle facades and dodge
the mirage from getting to
her breast and hips.

You are out of pocket if you
think love and logic can
coexist.
Ignorance is bliss.

Especially when past
relationships are dismissed
from lack of commitment.

Depicting the reason as to
why she's a pessimist.
Emotions resemble a
wrecking ship.
To her defense, she's the
cause for all her effects.

Leading to traumatic
events; leaving all feelings
interspersed like baggage
claim.

She claims that time
is moving backwards;

memories emulate a
matinee.

Late nights of lighting
thoughts that flash with no
filter.
Taking hundreds of selfies
just to make you feel better
in a world where you are
stereotyped.,
Plagiarized perceptions of
an essay you did not write.

I know you feel the pain, but
we must stay sane to sustain
those growing pains, those
growing pains.

The inner me fought for
freedom enticing my energy.
Vulnerability showed the real
me.
When I was a teen, I wore my
emotions on my sleeve.
Tommy Hill couldn't feel nor
figure the degree of those
heart burns, remembering
every lesson that I learned.

The truth can get
misconstrued; pick and
choose the company you
keep.
Iridescent features deplete
from silhouette hues.
Inflamed expectations left

my ego bruised,
It was conducive to follow
my own rules.

I had to feel the pain, I had
to stay sane to sustain my
growing pains. My growing
pains helped me change.

180

Changing views changes
you.
They don't want change
in you, but they give you a
reason to bring change in
you.
They see you've changed
then ask what's gotten into
you.

Ignoring the ignorance
caused the change in you.
No vein in my body routes
to vanity,
the insanity to be stuck in
the same thought mentality.

Counting your change, you
think it will give you some
sense?
Getting a glimpse of the
truth will rinse the lies off
your lips.

Used to think 360 was the
way to go, but you know
how it goes.
Thinking you're changing
but you're the same person
coming from a different
angle.

Stuck in a familiar spot
acting like the person you're
not.

Dizziness turns to confusion.
No understanding will have
your mind about to lose it.

The switch up was amazing,
no delays. My life has been
hitting 180's.
Rotating from the negativity
turned my back to those
that weren't feeling me.

Counting your change, you
think it will give you some
sense?
Getting a glimpse of the
truth will rinse the lies off
your lips.

Intermission

"If you could see what's coming, you wouldn't stress about what's happening."

September 11th

Feeling the cold breeze of a September day, except the breeze felt different this day. As a child not conformed to society but played hide and seek with anxiety and reality. In tune with the city that never sleeps.

This cold breeze shifted gravity.
This cold breeze caused agony.
This cold breeze collapsed time, as if the battery had a short fuse.
Filled with worry not knowing if this cold breeze took my mom.

Each second of the minute passes by. Hour hands unwind as husband and wives lost their lives. Frostbitten; numb to my existence. Forbidden thoughts couldn't express how I was feeling. This cold breeze put an ache in the crowns of connected wisdom. This cold breeze

slept the city that never
sleeps.

Seconds to None

The past is a blur
Present moment awareness
Future not promised.

Soul of the Wind

So much more meaning
in the words, the pen is
revealing all the pain that a
human being can sustain. I
do not know what is worse,
juggling time, money, and
women. Or the fact that I still
remember the scenes back
in November 2011, carrying
my brother in a hearse.

Man, that shit hurts;
reminiscing on his words. All
the real suffering happens
on this Earth. If time could
reverse, I would control the
break before making your
way home.

Heaven's angel overlooking
my steps and the angles that
my light illuminates; God
I am so thankful. So much
more meaning in my words.

Presence

Twenty-four hours
Each second and minute counts
Fulfill your purpose

Shadows of the Night

Shell capsules, soul and spirit
vacuumed from time.
Do not undermine energy,
eventually it could happen to you.

Death lurking, trapping people,
equal to life but living strife
disguise quiet nights as never-
ending flights of adrenaline.
Adrenal glands doped trying to
cope.

If it weren't for her demise, how
could I learn to live life? Feel the
pain in my eyes, is death the
opposite of daydreaming?

Compartmentalized emotions
spread faster than forest fire lies.
Sympathize over a thousand
times for a life.

Read between the lines, a
distraught image shadows the
night. Perception is a hit or miss;
you could be wrong or right.

Balance

Like the day and night,
Life is not immune to death.
Opposite attracts.

Mind Games

What if I told you that
depression triggered my
brain like an aneurysm to
the membrane?

Think about it...The one thing
that operates overheats
causing that feeling of
defeat; manufacturer cannot
complete.

Jabs to the body are
not menstrual; recycling
thoughts to your mental are
fearful.

Heart beats muted
emotions, instrumental.
FIGHT STILL, EVEN THOUGH
YOU ARE STUMBLING!

KEYS

Securing treasures,
Who are you to judge my
keys?
God is my locksmith.

What's the problem?

Positivity caused me to
be exalted, integrity flows
through my body and the
exhaust pipes to my drive is
never exhausted.

The calling on my life
interfered with distractions,
an anointed soul acted as an
ointment to my abrasions.

For a fool keeps making the
mistakes until you find the
root of your problems, you
think it's nonsense but you're
too prideful to acknowledge.

We complain about our
problems, but everyone has
problems. Which is a curse
wrapped in a gift.

Fast forward to the future
when you stop the repeat
of your problems; the old
test becomes the new
testament to the world of
poverty.

Note from 'Hapēnss

Pain is temporary.

Even though the burdens
from trials cloud your
judgement.
It may seem as though I am
distant.

The main factor is time.

The pain you felt time and
time again was not in vain.
It gave you the reassurance
to search me to find you.

Focus your energy,
I am immersed in every
strand of your DNA.

Sincerely,
Happiness

Reflections

We all have mirrors within
ourselves.

Can you look deep down
and see your own existence?

So why settle for less than
what your true high is?

Why only accept perfections
and hide your imperfections,
treating them like skeletons
to rot in your subconscious?

Decayed flesh of doubt
and fear discontinued heart
beats.

Blood, sweat, and tears
from hope that one day you
will believe in who you are,
perfectly being imperfect.

What's living if you hold your
high to captivity for a mere
reflection?
Shit, I am just living the high
before the high.

Unapologetically Black

Enriched Melanin,
dripped on my body from
God.
Self worth is priceless!

"Stop rewinding and fast forwarding your life, press play and experience who you are now."

Renovated Image

Renovate yourself when
you're going through pain,
Shattered images of your
innocence from a different
age.
Looking at your reflection,
recollecting your memory to
see what's changed.

Pieces from the past pass
through your life from a
decision you thought was
right.

Later suffered
consequences,
Overthinking got you
thinking over the fences.
Experimenting with your
fate,
Failing life's quizzes;
switching lenses disturbing
your vision.

Experience texted you the
answers, but you didn't get
the message.
Long nights have you feeling
restless, getting rest during
the lecture.
No pressure, learn to take

the punches and functions
when you have nothing.

Making myself stronger for
my next level; new age, new
opportunities.
Life is a movie and what you
show is a snippet; clip it to
your memory.
iCloud storage for all those
bottled-up emotions.

Different pics trying to
depict when I had the most
happiness.
Or when I was at my lowest
and nothing could cure it.
I just wanted to flourish.

Fresh 24

I have been patiently waiting
for my moment.
Chauffeured to my dream,
but it seems negativity has
my skeletons in a guillotine.
Anxiety arises but I'm
focused.
Melancholy, feeling lowly,
you couldn't see it in my
eyes, but my highs were
feeling wholly.

Blinded by astigmatism
vibes, curved visions
prophetic mind.
All we have is time; close
your eyes then it's vanished.

Living lavish I'm a savage
with a fresh 24.
Six seconds to score,
mamba mentality in the
fourth.
Reality will check your card;
stay on guard and know your
worth.

Defend your purpose.
Devils lurking
Can't control me
I was chosen.

No Limit

Jumping over the fence of
enlightenment.
feeling the immense power
of lightning desire.

Spoken words screaming to
my consciousness.
switching worlds with
another is an offense, you
must defend your higher.

Reaping the benefits, staying
prayed up to be prosperous;
God's angels spring clean
the skeletons in my closet.
Balance beams weighing
out my options.

Cannot be obnoxious,
frequencies frequently turn
into vivid lucid dreams.
My mind is elevated,
concentrated on what my
fate is.

Time is so expensive, too
expensive to be wasting.
Settling for minimum wage
cannot suffice any expenses.
Stay persistent even if it's
fourth and inches.

Those intangible traits
money couldn't replace.
Hard times we face; don't
you ever think your hustle
goes in vain.
Continuing to endure,
there's no limit to pain.

Energy

Your intuition never steered
you to lies,
Tuition is the issue lusting for
dollar bills to wipe the lid of
your eyes.

The enemy wants you
present on the front lines.
Your coping mechanisms
need to disappear, cloudy
judgments and flashy
demeanor.
Get hip to what you want to
do for the rest of your life.

Ships sink because it's
foundations weak
Gold links never break, look
at the diligent streak.

Pipes burst when the sink
overflows,
Same thing happens to your
mind when your thoughts
foreclose.

Look out for those
destroying their lives.
Freezing their hopes from
the negative vibes they give
off.

Energy transfers, so transfer
your energy to reach your
higher self.

To Be

Endure the struggle to reach
the next level,
Elevate to escape your
troubles.
The goal is far more valuable
than gold.

Do not fold, stop the crease.
Fate signed your lease,
worrying must cease
To be the person you want
to be.

Rewinding my thoughts to
the younger me,
carefree living free spirited
masterpiece.
Enrolled into my true form
gradually,
blessed to learn from those
that succeeded before me.

Casualties casually passed
down the torch,
The light is alive and ready
to take its course.

To be free; Break bonds
naturally. I just want to be
what I've been chosen to be.

Paths have been destined,
follow your heart. That's the
best lesson.
No profession could be
better than God's blessing.

Not doing what you've
chosen to be.
Arrest your ideas, you have
no idea what is ahead on
your journey.

To be free; Break bonds
naturally. I just want to be
what I've been chosen to be.

Joy Within

I will not allow anyone to
steal my joy,
For it is the light to my
darkness.
Uncertainty compels the
coyness in my responses.

Spreading throughout my
vessels, veins, and arteries.
Heart pumping honesty, no
lies from me,
Love is the pharmacy that
nurtures the physical body.

Love is patient.
Love is whole.
Love is consistent.
Love is overflowing.
Love is life.
Love is the air flowing to your
lungs.
Love is the essence of your
character.
Love is the message to your
cellular.

Love is what Love is.
Love is the flame to your
lighter when connection
sparks.
The opposite of love is love,

because hate is love from afar.

GOD IS LOVE!

Intuition

Intuition is ringing
Connections synced to my
thesis.
Flip the switch for
convenience,
Don't you drift off the deep
end.
Don't you drift off the deep
end.

Spark your brain like a lighter
that never loses its flame.
Feel your pain yearning
for highs, wondering why
wavelengths never die.
Close your eyes, find
your light; Living life is
understanding your light at a
distance.

One minute you're shining
from accomplishments,
Politicking with ya confidants
boosting their confidence.
Next second, dull
expressions from null
energies that cannot coexist.

Clarity is the same as
emptiness,
Clear to see when your

mental weighs less.
Reality is never permanent,
shifts to fit your every
second.

Bluetooth connected
interject opinions,
Who knew my truths
destroyed illusions?
Influence the youth helps
build their intuition.

Intuition is ringing
Connections synced to my
thesis.
Flip the switch for
convenience,
Don't you drift off the deep
end.
Don't you drift off the deep
end.

Conscious Actions

You must be right with your
left,
distinctive appearances to
activate the greatness you
possess.
Original described best; best
described as original.
See both ways. You know
to know who you are as an
individual.

Knowledgeable features
front row seats, you're not
the only one peeping.
Worldwide intuition puts
you at the location you were
destined to be.

Seeing the real and the fake;
knowing the outcome you
face.
Always listen; people reveal
their real intentions.

From the likes to the dislikes
that get you in and out of
the mood.
Gaining to maintain never
gets hooked into the loop.
Consistence and diligence
keep you on the straight and
narrow.

Your mind is the foundation
and consciousness
resembles the building.
Keep building your ideas to
skyscrape your dreams into
reality.

Securing Insecurities

Passionate to address your
passive aggression towards
love.
Push past the facades, Push
past the facades.

Whiplashed from trauma,
Flashback to when I was
abstract.
The women that I attracted
never resembled the
qualities of mama.
Actually, my reality was filled
with ill intent.

I want to love like it will break
generational curses.
Locked emotions banging
on corneas, forming running
waters.
Drowning from the
suppression of my ego's
demise.
Restless yearning to free the
mystery of irrational lies; told
on love.

The type of love that will
keep my mind focused on
a plethora of imperfections,
but reflections seem so
perfect.

Securing insecurities is
the cure for me, ensuring
honesty to the third degree.

That unconditional love is
what I'm conditioned for.
My word is bond, no terms
and conditions.

Letter 2 Love

Do you mind if I confide in
my truth?
Swallow my pride just for
you.
The game of Love has no
rules.

Love life stagnant like a
sprained ligament,
I used to always think friends
should have benefits.
Love lost in the times that
we are living in.

Early fantasies refuse to
stomach reality, fusing joint
personalities.
Confused parents' inflamed
discussions left their children
bruised.

Love, why are you so
challenging?
Miniscule infatuation, not
enough fuel to keep me
waiting.
Love has been complacent,
but I cannot fall into the
matrix.
Red pill can't keep the blues
off you, blue pill keeps the
affections pulsating.

Why do we abuse love's
valuable jewels?
Love has been a fuse as well
as poisonous fumes.
Spark my interests but
addicted to feelings, feeling
distant in the same room.

What's Your Flavor?

Through the night; armor
heavily knighted.
Don't try to fight it. I'm a
walking enigma.
Stay strong like our Black
queens, the vertebrae.
Different flavors may bend,
not break.

Black beauty queen
fantasizing over women
from Jet magazine.
Skin pixilation melanin
caramel complexion.
Stretch marks to guide me
to your soul. The next stop is
my destination.
Hearts racing facing bad
intentions with my hand
position.

No question on a quest to
find my flavor.
She's your counterpart and
the keys to your lanyard.
On my hip to get hip;
lips that's heaven sent,
personally elegant.

Your body is the chest to my
treasure,

Chest pumping hard
whenever my mind takes
over from the thought of
being together.
Do me a favor and tell me
what's your flavor.

Reciprocal

Unfolded affection loose
minds connected,
We have different worlds but
a common goal.
If you fall, I stumble because
I can't move without my
main vessel.
That's a lesson, there are
levels.

A limitless feeling that you
have a key to.
Cutting no corners, look over
your shoulders, undivided
attention.

We are blinded by
possibilities,
Muted affliction, fluent
actions corresponding to
intertwined emotions.

Reciprocal

A fiend for answers, love is a
hell of a drug.
Knowing you're my better
half; warm feelings when
you fill that hole.
Solid gold foundation
creating an empire.

Hands on the clock;
seconds to the day, and
minutes of the night.
Timeless experiences are a
recipe for life.

Reciprocal

Connections

Eye's glancing taking my
chances.
Patiently waiting for the day I
take her hand,
She will be my miss, never
missing the essence of
God's blessing.

Arresting her heart and
shortening breaths.
Hearts beating, I do. Is it true
that your loving, silhouetted
stress?

The day I approached her
was the day I followed love.
I finally had the heart to trust,
Cannot lie it was hard to
adjust.
For the first time this feeling
wasn't lust.
Before my perspective on
love was corrupt.

Until the day I approached
her...
My battery was dead, and
our connection gave me a
jump.

Amerikkkan Timez

What does it mean to be a
Black man in America?

A constant opinion from
the prejudice to who is the
fairest skin.
Where oppression
conceives fear,
Like a cigarette leaves debris
in the air.

We grieve from second
hand,
But fail to perceive the
obscene nature of the 45th
president.

Let me ask again.
What does it mean to be a
Black man in America?

We are fighting for 14% of
the wealth.
Where health care, student
loans, and pharmaceuticals
are the belt.
Lashing out the worst pain a
millennial has ever felt.

A lifetime has passed
and history repeats itself

verbatim.
The pride of America has
been forsaken.
How many degrees will we
receive before our actions
become vacant?
Young adolescents with
some sense trying to
decode the matrix.

Don't Shoot

There are unsolved
problems that we are
facing: fragile racists to
gentrification.
Can we destroy the false
perceptions of all races?
Or have a true meaning of
what race is.

Different cases have unfair
advantages.
Misplacing faces gets
missing from the face of the
Earth.

Black kings trying to live.
Vivid projections on how
they are still treating us.

Rest in paradise to the souls
killed before they could
make it to their goal.
For real, every murder is
getting recorded.
Highlight reel.

WITH MY HANDS UP,
"DON'T SHOOT, DON'T
SHOOT!!
MY MELANATED SKIN IS NOT
BULLETPROOF!!"

Justice or Just Us?

How am I supposed to feel?
Cops killing Blacks? Man it's
real.
Real life feeling like hell,
killing our motive.
No motion like they are
cutting our Achilles heel.

Surveillance surreal recurring
events,
CNN ignores social media,
vents to put their two cents
in.
Economics diminishing
and congress laughs at our
sufferings.
Passing mediocre bills;
poker faces bargaining their
millions and expanding their
ideas.

Erase racism off the face
of this Earth, first things first,
no debates - no justice no
peace.
We are the people, we know
what we need.

Support each other; then
boycott to rotten the
pockets of the obnoxious

white men.
Fighting to be united, living
in a country that fights to
earn its stripes.
I'm a Black king, a powerful
human being, but they fear
my life.

Divided races fall short of
being united.
Police striking; pour ice on
inflamed men committing
crimes with a title.

Where is JUSTICE? Feeling
like it is JUST US!

Liberty

Lady Liberty, let love last
longevity.
Lady Liberty, let love last
longevity.
Lady Liberty, let love last
longevity.

Hearts are heavy moving
through life steadily.
Louis' levees couldn't
leverage Katrina's feelings.
9/11 engraved from terrorists
with machetes.
Prejudice domestic
nationalist concealing their
intentions.
Lynchings from Tulsa
massacres, destroying
Black wall streets, setting us
backwards.

Corrupt systems preying on
the poor while the poor pray
for resources.
Seeing corpses lying fragile
from cop killings, caused
Kaepernick's kneeling.
Avoiding epidemics linked
to mental illnesses,
Poisonous profits killing
innocent civilians.

Treating Black lives like a
parody, Black prosperity is a
threat to white supremacy.

No coincidence, consider
this the beginning of
change.
Coins and cents to
rearrange self-reliance,
Create a space for
oppressors to face
consequences.
Coincide with sense from
generation to generation.

Lady Liberty, let love last
longevity.
Lady Liberty, let love last
longevity.
Lady Liberty, let love last
longevity.

Just A Thought

What if we weren't forced to
take a course to the coast?
Brothers linked together in
a boat.
Treated harshly, how did their
minds stay afloat?

Working free $.99 to incline
their time, undermining our
minds.
Blinded by the white man's
rights,
to do anything to survive,
right?

Fast forward to the 21st
century, lost traces of self-
identities.
Brothers make it to the jury
before their 21st.
Melanated kings carried by
loved ones escorted in a
hearse.

What is the use?
Tired of being a muse for
a country that misuse and
abuse
the image of me and
you, suffocating our
emancipation with a noose.

Food for thought, the fruit of
our labor has no flavor.
To bruise the system, we
must fuse each individual.
The clues have been written,
hieroglyphics from Martin,
Malcom, and DuBois.

WE ALL HAVE A VOICE,
Don't void the checks of our
ancestors.

Thank You God

On the road to riches, blue
and red lights in my rear
view.
Always be alert to the sign's
life be giving you.

No celebration, road rage to
success.
Heaven or hell, you choose
your destination.
I'm never devastated, using
negative outcomes as
inspiration.

Blessings over my head and
thanking the savior
For blinding me from the
ignorance of Satan.
Uncloaked intentions
plotting from the beginning.
If you're real, you'll realize
how to cut loose ends
to defend your natural
correlation.

Vivid projections are the
true meaning of what your
life's projecting.
Stay in your lane and excel
with jet fueled motivation.

I live a life simply to keep it
real and never forget to give
my 10%.
God makes smooth moves
waiting for you to put in
effort.
Doubling your worth while
giving you extra.

God I'm So Thankful!

The Essence of Time

A special angle, clear path,
no time for detours.
Angels collect my losses,
blessings disburse.
Time controls the mind like
the alarm to your reality.

Gears break, then your fears
are traced.
Once you're tuned into your
fate, real time takes place.

Parental advice for the
explicit features of life.
Multiple clocks that won't
tick, any second you can
lose it.
Minutes away from your
opportunity.

History of being unaware
affects timelines, loopholes
happen frequently.
Soliciting time undermines
minds.

When will we realize that
time is a valuable vendetta
of the world?

Volunteering vengeance,

time unmasking individuals.
Facing flashbacks are painful,
needing to cleanse a thing
or two.
Remembering that time you
were feeling vulnerable, it
took
time to get close to you.

Take responsibility to learn
from your injuries.
Just know that time heals
the hurt, but it also hurts to
heal.

Epilogue

We carry bags of unresolved emotional trauma; at times it could be self-inflicted from personal experiences or embedded in your DNA from your ancestors. Being triggered emotionally can be experienced involuntarily; even at the slightest stimulation, our brains tend to bring life to old situations we thought we had forgotten. I've been a victim of stress and anxiety where it has forced me to forget memories because it was associated with pain. At that time forgetting was the only way to escape unforeseen pain, not knowing that later it would be inevitable to experience that pain but with a greater intensity. Developing survival tactics that influenced my decision on how to cope with pain. Picking up the pieces may be perceived as a loss, but it allows you to become knowledgeable of your limitations and how much you can endure.

I had to unlearn the stereotypes of this world on a young Black king. One of the stereotypes was that vulnerability is equivalent to weakness and a luxury that many Black men cannot afford. I perceive being vulnerable as your ability to become aware of your emotions without being reactive. I soon found out that it would be my greatest strength by becoming my authentic self, releasing from the chokehold of expectations of others and the need for their validation. Our egos are only a mere reflection of expectations to conform to society.

When you have accepted the lessons from your trials and allowed your soul to cleanse then you will experience self-love. There is no time limit to healing nor is healing linear, but moving forward will only aid in your growth. The process of healing can be prolonged with setbacks from feeling numb, sulking with your pain to feel it again, which can be addictive. Healing doesn't mean that your pain never existed, it only means that the pain no longer has control over your life. Your pain does not define who you are, but instead your willingness to help transform others with your pain.

Without God, this publication would not have been possible.

Stephen G. Norman was born in Brooklyn, NY and raised in Wake Forest, NC. He graduated Cum Laude from the illustrious North Carolina Central University with a degree in Athletic Training. Stephen has always been a man of many talents, from teaching himself how to play the saxophone to becoming a business owner. Although writing was never in his plans,he impulsively started writing poetry after his junior year of undergrad, which ultimately led to his authorial debut, *The Essence of Time*.

Instagram: _therealstephenG
Twitter: _stephenG7